AF408596

The Rainbow Inside You: A Journey Through the Chakras

Printed in USA

Independent Publishing
Cover design by Denisse Zapata
First Edition: May, 2024

For permissions or inquiries, please contact the Author at info@littlealchemytales.com

From the tapestry of my motherhood to the unfolding chapters of yours!

From the ethereal font of my odyssey through the realms of motherhood, a saga unfurls - a tapestry interlaced with strands of divine enlightenment and personal revelations.

Within the nurturing cradle of motherhood, I discovered a profound joy in bestowing upon my progeny the sacred wisdom that they transcend mere mortal coil and cognition. They are celestial spirits, luminous entities with boundless vistas of potential. Embracing this timeless truth, they entwine with their celestial core and boundless wisdom, where their limitless dreams and unique gifts illuminate their journey, weaving a spell of wonder and reverence upon their existence.

Bound by love and luminescence,

Denisse

Once upon a time, a curious little boy named Noah lived in a land filled with magic and wonder. He loved to explore the world around him and discover its many secrets. One day, while playing in his grandmother's garden, he found an old, sparkling book. "What's this?" he wondered, opening the cover. He found a message: "Noah, you have a rainbow inside you. Let's find it together!"

Noah ran to his grandmother, holding the book. "Grandma, it says I have a rainbow inside me! Is it true?" His grandmother smiled warmly and said, "Yes, Noah. You have seven special lights called chakras. They shine like a rainbow inside you. Close your eyes, and we'll go on a magical journey to find them."

GRANDMA
GRANDMA

Noah closed his eyes and took a deep breath. Suddenly, he found himself in a beautiful, enchanted forest. In front of his were seven sparkling lights, each a different rainbow color.

The first light glowed a deep, rich red. "I am the Root Chakra," it said soothingly. "I help you feel safe and strong, just like the roots of a mighty tree." Noah felt the earth beneath his feet, solid and comforting, and he smiled.

Next, an orange light shimmered warmly. "I am the Sacral Chakra," it whispered joyfully. "I bring you joy and creativity, like painting pictures or dancing to music." Noah twirled around, feeling happiness bubble up inside him.

A radiant yellow light appeared next. "I am the Solar Plexus Chakra," it announced brightly. "I give you confidence and courage like a shining sun lighting the day." Noah stood tall and proud, feeling the warmth and power of the sun within him.

A gentle green light began to glow. "I am the Heart Chakra," it sang softly. "I help you love deeply and be kind, like a warm, comforting hug." Noah wrapped his arms around himself, feeling a tender, loving warmth spread through his chest.

A serene blue light shimmered into view. "I am the Throat Chakra," it spoke gently. "I help you speak your truth and listen carefully, like the sweet song of a bird," Noah whispered kind words into the breeze and listened to the gentle rustling of the leaves.

A deep indigo light twinkled like a distant star. "I am the Third Eye Chakra," it said softly. "I help you see clearly and imagine wonderful things, like a wise owl at night." Noah closed his eyes and saw beautiful dreams and bright ideas dancing in his mind.

Finally, a soft violet light glowed above him. "I am the Crown Chakra," it whispered. "I connect you to the stars and the universe like a crown of light guiding you." Noah felt a gentle, peaceful connection to everything around him as if he were part of the stars.

Noah opened his eyes, feeling the colors of the rainbow shining brightly inside him. "Thank you, Grandma," he said, hugging her tightly. "Now I know my inner rainbow and its magic!"

Grandma smiled and said, "Remember, Noah, whenever you feel lost or sad, just close your eyes, take a deep breath, and find your rainbow. It's always there to guide you and bring you joy."

And so, Noah lived happily ever after, always remembering the magical rainbow inside him. With the beautiful colors of his chakras shining bright, he spread love, joy, and kindness wherever he went.

The End.

About the Author

In the mystical lands of the Andes in Lima, Perú, emerged Denisse N. Zapata, embarking on a celestial odyssey at the tender age of 26. Her soul's yearning for profound truths kindled a metamorphosis, leading her to illuminate the path for mothers and their precious offspring.

Within the tapestries of her "little alchemy tales," Denisse weaves spells of tenderness, empathy, and mindfulness, nurturing the sacred bond between parent and child. Her sacred mission unfolds as she empowers families, sowing seeds of spiritual awakening and forging connections with the ethereal realms.

Through the alchemy of workshops and personal guidance, Denisse harmonizes spiritual wisdom with holistic well-being, birthing sanctuaries where families bloom. Her unwavering commitment serves as a beacon, uniting a tribe of enlightened mothers and children, reveling in the splendor of shared voyages and the boundless magic dwelling within each soul.